Sunshine Coast

FRASER ISLAND   NOOSA   MOOLOOLABA   CALOUNDRA

Peter Lik

Additional Photography:
Paul Ewart

PETER LIK

"My total dedication and obsession with photography has taken me on journeys into many remarkable areas throughout Australia.
I captured this collection of images using a specialist panoramic camera. Because of the wider field of view, this format enables me to portray the true spirit of Australia on film. Upon viewing these images I am sure you will share with me the tranquillity and solitude I experienced whilst exploring the stunning beauty of this country."

PETER LIK PUBLISHING (SEQ)

South East Queensland Wholesale Enquiries:

Peter Lik Publishing (SEQ)
PO Box 520 New Farm Qld 4005
Phone: 61 7 3303 9966 Fax: 61 7 3303 9969
Email: paul.ewart@mac.com

Wholesale Enquiries (Australia except South East Queensland):

Lifestyle Music Pty Ltd
PO Box 1 Babinda Qld 4861
Phone: 61 7 4067 5300 Fax: 61 7 4067 5390
Email: orders@lifestyleentertainment.com.au

music words pictures play

© **Peter Lik Publishing** (SEQ) 2009 BK17

ISBN 1 876 5850 56

Front cover - Alexandra Bay, Noosa National Park.
Additional photography - Paul Ewart www.travpix.com, www.Viewfinder.com.au

Designed and produced in Australia by Peter Lik Publishing.
Printed in China by Everbest.

SUNSHINE COAST

One of Australia's regions of unsurpassed beauty, Queensland's Sunshine Coast is just an hours' drive north of Brisbane. Still largely unspoilt and carefully protected, the area's sparkling beaches, shining waterways and restful mountains provide a haven for locals and visitors alike. A backdrop of green, forested mountains and rich volcanic plains slope down to the warm waters of the Pacific Ocean.

Kilometres of white sandy beaches offer world-class surfing, and every kind of water activity under the sun. For anglers, experienced or novice, few places in Australia can match the variety of year-round fishing. Explore the beachside resort towns of Coolum, Maroochydore, Mooloolaba and Caloundra—each with their own character and appeal. For fine dining, shopping and accommodation Noosa is the place. Bordered by surfing beaches, national parks and inland waterways the sophistication of Noosa is surprisingly unspoilt.

Thousands of hectares of national parks lie within the Sunshine Coast region. Explore ancient palm groves, rainforest and wet eucalypt forest. Noosa National Park, with its protected coves, has a network of walking trails with panoramic seascapes.

The world's largest sand island, the World Heritage-listed Fraser Island is close by. Take a 4WD tour and discover towering sand blows, ancient rainforests and inland freshwater lakes.

The nearby Hinterland is home to the Glasshouse Mountains, diverse horticultural areas and friendly mountain villages. Montville, Maleny, Flaxton and Mapleton attract some of the world's most creative talents. Browse amongst the quality galleries, craft shops and weekend markets. Queensland's Sunshine Coast is the perfect place for a perfect holiday.

SUNSHINE

A bird's eye view of the shifting sands at the mouth of the Noosa River that create idyllic conditions for boating.

 # NOOSA

One of the best loved beach resorts in Australia, Noosa has managed to develop into an international standard destination, while retaining its original beach holiday charm.

Some visitors are content to not venture much further afield than the relaxed ambience of the beach and Hastings Street, with its cosmopolitan mix of beachfront dining, buzzing cafes, elegant shopping and award-winning restaurants. As well though, there's an abundance of natural beauty to explore in the area.

Noosa's golden, sun-drenched beaches are among the finest in Australia. The three main beaches, Noosa Main Beach, Alexandria Bay and Sunshine Beach are complemented by many other picturesque bays and coves. The area has become a mecca for surfers searching for the perfect wave, with sweeping breaks custom made for long boarding.

The Noosa River has more than 40km of navigable waterways, and at every turn there's something unique and beautiful to discover.

Nearby are the hinterland villages of Eumindi and Yandina and the untouched wilderness of the Cooloola Coast, stretching for 50km between Noosa and Fraser Island – the largest sand island in the world.

The 54,000 hectare Cooloola National Park is a spectacular wilderness area with long sandy beaches, mangrove-lined waterways, forests, heaths and lakes.

N O O S A

Previous page: Lapped by the gentle waters of Laguna Bay, Main Beach hugs the length of Noosa's Hastings Street.

NOOSAVILLE

The Noosa River has more than 40km of navigable waterways.
Along the river, Noosaville retains its own distinct character.
Colourful boat hire outlets line the riverfront where children swim
in the shallows off the sandy banks. The adjoining wide parkland
is the perfect spot for joggers, picnickers and walkers.

 COOLOOLA

The birthplace of the Noosa River is Cooloola. The tannin stained upper waters create magnificent reflections (right) as the river slows through dense banks lined with sedges. The river passes through the Cooloola National Park and past Kinaba National Park and enters Lake Cootharaba, Queensland's largest natural lake.

Dawn over Weyba Creek.

Within Cooloola National Park is an impressive array of unusual flora and fauna.

The sheer beauty of nature's creation at Rainbow Beach and Double Island Point.

Seventy-two colours of sand can be found in cliffs of up to 200 metres.

Sand is the dominating feature of World Heritage-listed Fraser Island, developed over 800,000 years. Australia's purest breed of dingoes exists here together with wallabies, possums and echidnas. The island is also home to crystal clear creeks, remarkable rainforests and perched lakes.

The pristine waters of Lake McKenzie, one of Fraser Island's largest freshwater lakes.

COOLUM
Aerial view of Coolum, with Mount Coolum (left) in the background.

The natural, unspoilt beauty of Coolum Beach.

COOLUM

Coolum

Just 20 minutes south of Noosa, Coolum is a favourite holiday spot for families who love the village atmosphere, safe swimming and spectacular views. Coolum is also home to several international-standard resorts and one of the most popular events on the Australian golfing calendar, the Australian PGA Tour Coolum Classic. Golfers can tee off on world-class golf courses including Hyatt Regency Coolum, Novotel Twin Waters and nearby Noosa Springs and Pelican Waters. Head to Coolum village for its cosmopolitan mix of cafes, bars and restaurants or take the new boardwalk (above right) which offers easy access between the main beach and nearby secluded coves. The village is set against the backdrop of Mount Coolum, a popular destination for bushwalkers and nature lovers.

 # MAROOCHY

Located in the heart of the beautiful Sunshine Coast, the Maroochy Shire is one of Australia's most enticing holiday destinations.

Its first Aboriginal inhabitants named the area Marutchi, which means `red bill', the name of the black swan. European settlement followed in the late 19th century, with Maroochy Shire gazetted in 1890.

Today locals and holidaymakers enjoy the best of both worlds. The coastal resort towns of Mooloolaba, Alexandra Headland and Coolum to the north each have their own character and style.

Maroochy is home to some of Australia's most famous beaches, including Mooloolaba, Alexandra Headland, Coolum and Maroochydore, their golden sands washed by the warm waters of the Pacific Ocean. The beautiful Maroochy River is the area's natural centrepiece, a paradise for anglers and water sports enthusiasts. An eco cruise is the best way to explore the river's thriving birdlife and 200 year old mangroves.

A short drive inland is the unspoilt appeal of the magnificent Sunshine Coast Hinterland. Take the time to explore the charming villages of the Blackall Ranges and pristine rainforests. The quaint English-style village of Montville is home to fabulous restaurants and cafes, craft shops, boutiques and galleries.

With an average seven hours of sunshine per day and an average daily temperature of between 24 and 25 degrees celsius, Maroochy's sub-tropical climate is well suited to a relaxed, outdoor lifestyle and holiday fun.

There are plenty of perfect spots for a barbecue or picnic, while surfing, sailing and fishing are the most popular water activities to be enjoyed year round. From the beautiful beaches to the lush farmland, mountain ranges and spectacular rainforests, there's something for everyone.

ALEXANDRA

The ideal spot to catch an early morning wave.

HEADLAND

M O O L O

 # Mooloolaba

Stretching from Alexandra Headland to Point Cartwright, Mooloolaba has undergone a stunning transformation during the past couple of years. Yesterday's sleepy beachfront of surf shops and hamburger joints has been replaced with a stylish, cosmopolitan beachside resort town. Elegant resorts and apartments, al fresco restaurants, deli's, cafes and designer boutiques line the beachfront boulevard. Located by the Mooloolah River, Mooloolabah boasts coastal and river frontages. Mooloolaba is named for 'mulu', the Aboriginal word for schnapper fish, or 'mulla' the red-bellied black snake. Originally called Mooloolah Heads, the name was changed to Mooloolaba by Thomas O'Connor who sub-divided land for sale there.

LOO WITH A VIEW
(right) One of Mooloolaba's most quirky attractions is the "Loo with a View". Featuring an absolute beachfront location and million dollar views, the world famous "loo" offers a spectacular viewing platform, change room and facilities.

NEXT PAGE: Visit UnderWater World for close encounters with dangerous sharks, huge gropers and stingrays.

Caloundra City

Long a favourite destination for Australian holiday makers, Caloundra City is the southern gateway to Queensland's beautiful Sunshine Coast.

Located just 91km north of Brisbane, Caloundra stretches across 1,102 square kilometres from the green coastal hinterland to the Pacific Ocean, creating a picture perfect playground for those who enjoy the best nature offers. It's no wonder the Aboriginal meaning for Caloundra is 'beautiful place'.

A period of exciting growth has recently transformed Caloundra, with multi-million-dollar resorts, vibrant new restaurants, cafes and conference centres springing up around the city.

While the transformation has created a more sophisticated holiday destination, Caloundra's relaxed and friendly lifestyle remains one of its biggest assets. With an average seven hours of sunshine daily and mild winters, life here is geared around the outdoors.

From Golden Beach in the south to Buddina in the north, there are 10 beautiful beaches for locals and visitors to enjoy. Caloundra City itself is encircled by no less than six main beaches, several of which are renowned for their excellent surfing breaks.

Bribie Island's long northern sandbar forms a natural shelter, creating the calm waters of Pumicestone Passage and nearby Bulcock and Golden Beaches, which are top spots for windsurfing, boating and fishing.

Just a short drive west is the peaceful Hinterland - here you'll find another world of charming country villages, tropical fruit plantations and lush rainforest, set against the dramatic backdrop of the spectacular volcanic Glass House Mountains. Steeped in history, the mountains carry Aboriginal names but were collectively named by explorer Captain James Cook in 1770.

There are peaceful National Parks and nature reserves to explore all within easy access from the heart of Caloundra, or while away the hours in the many arts and crafts shops, tuck into a Devonshire tea or browse your way through the colourful country markets.

But best of all, Caloundra has retained the laidback atmosphere of a small coastal town, as one of Queensland's favourite holiday spots.

CALOUNDRA CITY

AUSTRALIA ZOO
Australia Zoo is home to the world famous Steve Irwin, the "Crocodile Hunter" and his family, along with more than 550 animals and an interactive children's zoo.

The sun's last rays light the awesome Glass House Mountains (this page and overleaf). Rising above the patchwork of tropical fruit plantations, the 10 volcanic monoliths of the Glass House Mountains were formed 24 million years ago, and are shrouded in Aboriginal legend.

The fertile volcanic soil surrounding the Glass House Mountains is ideal for small crop
agriculture, especially tropical fruits such as pineapples, lychees, avocados and strawberries.

 # Hinterland

Just a short drive from Caloundra, the Sunshine Coast's Hinterland invites leisurely exploration. The scenery is spectacular, from the views of the dramatic Glass House peaks to the Blackall Ranges, 450 metres above sea level and home to the mountain villages of Maleny, Montville, Flaxton and Mapleton. Take the time to discover the host of cosy country retreats, galleries, restaurants, wineries and interesting shops.

Mary Cairncross Scenic Reserve near Maleny features some of the last remaining natural rainforest in South East Queensland. The peaceful reserve comprises more than 50 hectares of subtropical rainforest and 2.5km of boardwalks and walking trails.

Lake Baroon is the main water supply for Caloundra and Maroochy, and a popular spot for swimming, fishing, sailing and canoeing.

Maleny remains a working dairy town, although it is fast becoming recognised as a haven for artists who create a fascinating variety of arts and crafts. Its rolling green hills and deep pockets of rainforest offer a peaceful alternative to the coastal strip.

The cooler Hinterland climate is perfect for al fresco dining, and cosy fireside meals in the winter months,
with dining choices ranging from Devonshire teas to hearty country fare and á la carte.

The University of the Sunshine Coast Library is renowned for its distinctive, sub-tropical architecture. The building opened in 1997, and in the same year, was awarded the prestigious Sir Zelman Cowen Award for Public Buildings.

Peter Lik - The Photographer

Peter Lik is one of the world's most innovative and prolific landscape photographers. His passion and dedication to his craft are unsurpassed, and Peter is recognised as the leader in his field.

He was born in Melbourne, Australia in 1959, the only son of Czech immigrant parents. Completely self taught, Peter's talent for photography was evident from an early age. He first picked up a camera at the age of eight, and has retained a spirit and enthusiasm for his work that is equalled only by his unbounded energy and deep affinity for the land. It was whilst travelling in Alaska in 1994 that Peter's fascination with photography took a dramatic turn. Previously only working with 35mm cameras, he discovered the encompassing view of the panoramic camera and he was converted. It opened up a whole new world of creative possibilities and took him to another level in his photography.

In 1997 Peter took the courageous step of entering the competitive world of publishing with the birth of Peter Lik Publishing. He began with specialised panoramic postcards and the range of small hard cover books that have become his trademark. His first large format coffee table book "Australia – Images of a Timeless Land" is a stunning showcase of Peter's most emotive images. Now in its fourth reprint, the book received the prestigious "Galley Award" for excellence in production. Peter's latest publications are the magnificent "Spirit of America" and "Maui - Hawaiian Paradise".

The success of his publishing company provided Peter with the platform to fulfil a lifelong dream of opening his own galleries selling limited editions of his work. He opened his first gallery in his hometown of Cairns and due to an overwhelming demand, it was followed almost immediately by a second in Port Douglas.

Now with further galleries in Sydney, Noosa, Hawaii and Las Vegas, Peter Lik has established a credible presence worldwide. With handcrafted local timber floors and unique custom designed furniture, his galleries radiate a beautiful ambience and are a fitting environment in which to profile his work.

Peter's artistic landscapes have been recognised with a growing list of awards. The Australian Institute of Professional Photography (AIPP) has honoured his talents with their highest accolades. As an investment opportunity, Peter's images are increasing in value as respect and recognition for his work spreads throughout the world.